18

QUEEN'S GATE
JUNIOR SCHOOL

Catching a Meal

Paul Bennett

Wayland

Nature's Secrets

Catching a Meal
Changing Shape
Hibernation
Making a Nest
Migration
Pollinating a Flower

Cover: A male archer fish catches his prey by leaping out of the water for his prize! Sometimes archer fish spit at flies or other insects so that they fall into the water.
Title page: A common kingfisher perches on a branch to eat a fish.
Contents page: A strand of silk with a blob of glue on the end dangles from a bolas spider.

Series editor: Francesca Motisi
Book editor: Francesca Motisi
Designer: Joyce Chester
Consultant: Stephen Savage
Stephen Savage provided the notes for parents and teachers.

First published in 1994 by
Wayland (Publishers) Ltd
61 Western Road, Hove
East Sussex BN3 1JD, England

© Copyright 1994 Wayland (Publishers) Ltd

British Library Cataloguing in Publication Data

Bennett, Paul
  Catching a Meal. (Nature's Secrets Series)
  I. Title II. Series
  591.53

ISBN 0-7502-1063-X

Printed and bound in Italy by
G. Canale & C.S.p.A., Turin

Picture acknowledgements
The publishers would like to thank the following for allowing their photographs to be reproduced in this book: Bruce Coleman Ltd *cover* (Kim Taylor), 4 (below/Kim Taylor), 5 (above/Frank Greenaway, below/Kim Taylor), 7 (top/Gunter Ziesler), 13 (Kim Taylor), 16 (Kim Taylor), 20 (above/Gerald Cubitt, below/Dr Frieder Sauer), 21 (above/Dr Rocco Longo). 23 (main/Felix Labhardt), 28 (Kim Taylor), 29 (above/Kim Taylor, below/John Shaw); Frank Lane Picture Agency 17 (top/Silvestris, below/Eric & David Hosking); the Natural History Photographic Agency *contents page* (A.N.T.), 4 (above/Christophe Ratier), 7 (middle/Stephen Krasemann), 9 (Robert Erwin), 10 (Stephen Dalton), 17 (middle/Silvestris Fotoservice), 21 (below/Anthony Bannister), 22 (above/Stephen Dalton, below/A.N.T.), 27 (above/ Bill Wood); Oxford Scientific Films Ltd 6 (Waina Cheng), 7 (bottom/Steve Turner), 8 (above/Mary Stouffer Animals Animals, below/David C Fritts Animals Animals), 11 (below/Frank Huber), 12 (below/Norbert Rosing), 18 (above/Howard Hall), 19 (Tony Tilford), 24 (above/Tom McHugh, below/Howard Hall), 25 (above/Carl Roessler Animals Animals, below/Fred Bavendam), 26 (Fred Bavendam), 27 (below/Colin Milkins); Survival Anglia 11 (above/Jeff Foott), 12 (above/Alan Root), 15 (below Bruce Davidson), 18 (below/Dieter & Mary Plage).

Contents

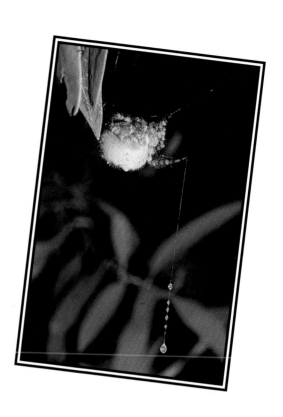

Introduction

All animals need food to stay alive. Most humans can go shopping for food, but other animals must catch their own meals. Some animals can eat plants, but carnivores are unable to digest plants, so they must eat meat. But it is not an easy meal when you have to catch it first!

◁ This cheetah is chasing after a small gazelle. It can run as fast as 96 kph, but only over 400 m or so. If it has not caught its prey within that distance it has to give up.

An earth worm makes a tasty mouthful for this song thrush. The thrush pulled the worm quickly out of the ground using its slim bill. ▷

△ Many frogs like to catch and eat insects. This common frog is cleverly catching a meal by shooting out its tongue.

Some plants do not get the goodness they need from the soil and so they must catch animals too. This great bladderwort has caught a mosquito larva. ▷

Mammals

Animals either hunt alone or together in packs to help them catch larger prey. Lions use many different methods of hunting, but it is usually a lioness who makes the kill.

△ A lion and lioness are stealthily approaching their prey so that they can get close enough to leap on it.

△ They have been
spotted by a zebra and it
runs away. The lioness
immediately gives chase.

She has caught the zebra
and the rest of the pride
arrive quickly to kill the
zebra. ▷

Lions, like other
flesh-eating
mammals, have
long, pointed
canine teeth for
biting their prey. ▷

△ The agile bobcat likes to eat birds and small animals, but it can bring down a deer by leaping on to its back. Here it is chasing after a snowshoe hare.

Large, lumbering bears are not swift enough to catch deer. Instead they like to eat roots, berries and small animals. Most, like this brown bear, love to eat fish – they stand in the water and wait for some tasty fish to swim by. ▷

△ Stoats are fearsome hunters. They are very agile and can catch and kill animals larger than themselves, such as this rabbit. This stoat has changed from its brown summer coat to white, so that is camouflaged in the snow.

◁ Many bats emit high-pitched bursts of sound which bounce back to them off objects around them. This is called echo-location. This greater horseshoe bat is swooping to catch a juicy moth by using echo-location.

Otters have powerful tails and webbed feet for swimming speedily after fish. Sea otters like to dive for shellfish which they skilfully crack open on a small rock balanced on their tummies. ▷

◁ A Steller's sea lion enjoys a meal of delicious salmon. Sea lions have strong flippers to enable them to swim as fast as the fish they hunt.

Reptiles and amphibians

Tortoises, crocodiles and snakes are all reptiles. Amphibians include frogs, newts, toads and salamanders. Many of these creatures swim well and are fierce hunters.

◁ A crocodile lies threateningly in wait for animals to come down to the water to drink.

It has fearsome-looking teeth for seizing its prey. ▽

A giant chameleon catches an unlucky
fly. It has a long tongue which it shoots
out in the blink of an eye. The tongue
has a sticky grasping tip for catching
its prey.

The horned frog from South America
will eat almost anything it can catch.
Its huge mouth allows it to swallow a
mouse whole.

△ Poisonous snakes will kill, paralyse or blind a victim with their venom (poison). The fangs of this rattlesnake are like hypodermic needles for injecting venom into its victim.

Not all snakes are venomous. Constricting snakes stealthily ambush their prey, throw their coils around it and powerfully squeeze it to death. This African python is starting to swallow a squirrel. ▷

Birds

A huge number of birds are insect-eaters and have slender bills. Others can kill large prey or like to eat fish.

△ A barn owl swoops silently to catch a helpless mouse. The owl has very soft feathers, which allow it to fly almost silently as it hunts its prey in the dark of the night.

The kingfisher perches motionless on a branch until it spots a fish.

△ In a flash, it plunges into the water and takes the fish. ▷

It returns to the branch and will swallow the fish head first. ▷

With their flipper-like 'wings', these Galapagos penguins 'fly' through a shoal of delicious fish. ▽

◁ The clever woodpecker finch winkles out fat grubs from under the bark of a tree using a tool such as a cactus spine.

The flamingo has a special bill for filtering foods such as algae, snails and tiny animals from the water. It holds its bill in an upside-down position. ▷

Insects and spiders

Killer mini-beasts use all kinds of ways to catch a meal, including chasing, traps, webs and pouncing.

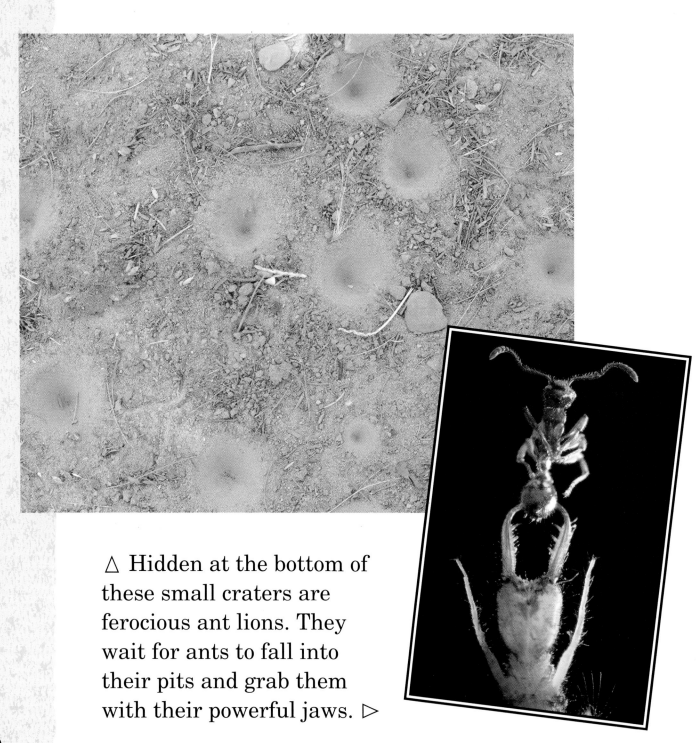

△ Hidden at the bottom of these small craters are ferocious ant lions. They wait for ants to fall into their pits and grab them with their powerful jaws. ▷

△ The praying mantis is a fierce killer of insects and spiders. It holds its arms raised as if praying before pouncing on its victim.

Brightly-coloured ladybirds feast on juicy aphids. The ladybirds' colouring warns birds that they are not good to eat. ▷

△ A jumping spider leaps on to a fly.

◁ A net-casting spider will catch any small insect that passes underneath with its small web.

The delicate web of a garden spider will trap flying insects. (*Inset*) A strand of silk with a blob of glue on the end dangles from a bolas spider. The spider hopes to catch a moth with it. ▷

Fish and sea creatures

The smell of blood in the water will attract hungry sharks from all directions. This black-tip reef shark is feeding on a mackerel. ▽

◁ Not all sharks are dangerous to people. A basking shark glides through the water with its huge mouth open to catch tiny plankton.

△ A cleaner wrasse 'cleans' a bright
red big eye fish by eating parasites.

Like a fisherman,
an angler fish uses
its worm-shaped
lure to attract prey.
As the prey comes
near, the well-
camouflaged angler
fish snaps it up in
its huge mouth. ▷

Octopuses are active hunters. Their tentacles grab the prey which is killed by a bite from the octopus's deadly beak. This Pacific giant octopus is feeding on a dead dogfish shark.

△ Corals with vivid-yellow stinging tentacles around the mouth have stunned a fish that has come too close.

Some creatures catch a meal by filtering particles of food from water. An orbshell cockle uses its delicate tube-like siphon to draw in food. ▷

Plants

Some plants that live on poor soils find nourishment by catching small insects.

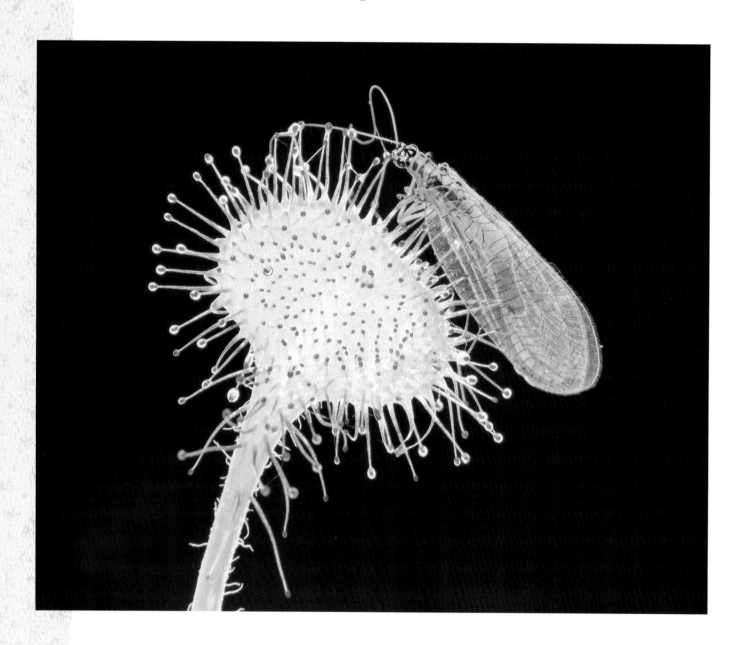

△ The sundew has leaves with sticky 'hairs' which trap the insects that land on them. The leaf closes over the insect as it is digested.

△ A dazzling damselfly is about to trigger the leaf of a Venus fly-trap. Once closed, the insect cannot escape.

The tube-like leaves of the pitcher plant collect rainwater. A sweet smell from the leaves attracts insects, which slide helplessly down the tube and drown. ▷

Glossary

Algae A group of plants that can live in water.

Amphibians Animals that are adapted to live on land and in water.

Camouflaged An animal that is disguised so that is not easily seen against its background.

Canine One of the four pointed teeth, one on each side of the upper and lower jaws.

Carnivores Meat-eating animals or plants.

Digest To break up food in the stomach and turn it into a form which the body can use.

Emit To give out.

Hypodermic needle Fine, hollow needle for giving injections into the skin.

Insect Any small, six-legged creature with a body divided into sections and usually with wings.

Lure Something that attracts; bait.

Mammals Animals whose females give birth to live young which they feed with milk from their bodies.

Packs Groups of animals of the same kind.

Paralyse To make helpless; loss of movement and feeling.

Parasites Animals that live on other animals from which they obtain nourishment.

Plankton Very tiny creatures (including animals and plants) floating in the sea.

Prey Animals killed by others for food.

Reptiles Animals, such as lizards, snakes, or turtles, which have a backbone and a scaly skin. They are cold-blooded and usually fully adapted to living on land.

Siphon A tube for drawing off something.

Books to read

Discovering Nature series
(Wayland Publishers Ltd):
A series of books that takes
a wide look at animals and
plants. It includes titles on
bats, birds of prey, bugs,
freshwater fish, frogs and
toads, jellyfish, otters, owls,
saltwater fish, seabirds,
snakes and lizards, spiders
and weasels.
Crocodiles by Norman
Barrett (Franklin Watts,
1989)
Big Cats by Norman Barrett
(Franklin Watts, 1989)
Life Story: *Bear* by Mike
Down (Eagle Books, 1993)
The Wolf by Jeremy
Bradshaw (Boxtree, 1991)

Notes for parents and teachers

Project: **Catching Food**

Keep a diary of any animals you observe
catching their food. Look for orb spiders'
webs in and around your garden. These
sticky webs are ideal for catching flying
insects. Keep a note of the number of
insects that are caught in a day. Name any
insects that you recognize.

Some wild animals are used to living
near people. You may be lucky to see these
animals more clearly by putting food out
for them. High in the sky you may see
birds of prey hunting for food. If you live
near the coast, you may see seabirds
diving for fish. Domestic cats sometimes
use their hunting instincts to catch small
birds and mice. Make a note of your
observations.

Project: **Crabs and Anemones**

Crabs and sea anemones catch their food
in very different ways. You can set up a
temporary aquarium to observe how they
feed. Cover the bottom of the aquarium
with gravel and put in a pile of rocks so
that the crabs can climb out of the water.
Fill the aquarium about two thirds full
with sea water, or use artificial sea water
from an aquarium shop. You will also need
an air pump.

Visit your local shoreline and catch a
few crabs with a net. Find a small rock or
sea shell that has sea anemones growing
on it. Avoid touching the tentacles as sea
anemones sting their prey. Place them in
the aquarium. Carefully drop some food
into the anemones' tentacles and watch
how they feed. Watch the crabs use their
claws and mouth parts for eating. Keep a
diary of your observations. If you do not
live near the coast you could set up an
aquarium for freshwater crayfish and
other freshwater life.

Places to visit: You may see some of the
animals from this book in a zoo, aquarium
or nature park.

Index